Holy Spirit Ignored No More

A Formal Introduction To the God in You

Daryl W. Arnold

REV/12 PUBLICATIONS

Holy Spirit Ignored No More: A Formal Introduction To The Holy Spirit

Rev/12 Publishing
211 Harriet Tubman Street
Knoxville, TN 37915
www.overcomingbelieverschurch.org
office@overcomingbelieverschurch.org
(865) 633-9050

ISBN: 9781096338895
Independently published

Printed in the United States of America

ACKNOWLEDGEMENTS

There is an old story that is told that says if you ever see a turtle sitting on top of a fence you would be a fool to think that he got there on his own. Turtles don't climb fences. Someone had to help him get that high. Only a fool would think that the youngest of five children raised by a single parent could get to this place without assistance. I want to acknowledge a few people who God has ordained to be in my life that have helped me become who I am in Christ.

To my momma Cladie Arnold who spent her entire life sacrificing for her children so that they could become all that God wanted them to be. Thank you, Momma, for every word of encouragement, correction and even rebuke that you gave me. I am who I am because you are who you are.

To my wife Carmeisha who is the rib that covers my heart, the epitome of a virtuous woman and the greatest example of a mother that I have ever witnessed. Thank you for your unconditional love and patience with me even when I was not as patient with you. You have been the bridge that God has used to take me over every obstacle that life has presented me.

To my children, Daisha, Chania, Timberland and Azariah. The Bible says that you are the inheritance of the Lord and I agree. You have been four of the greatest gifts that God has given me. Thank you for living in the shadows of ministry and yet maintaining your love for the Lord.

To my Spiritual family Overcoming Believers Church (OBC), who has been the pillar of our community and a City that is set upon a hill for many, many years. Thank you for all of your investments into the vision that the Lord has given me. You have followed by faith and have made undeniable impacts in the city of Knoxville and around the globe. May the Father make you rich in every area of your life and add no sorrow.

To Calvin "Pop" Hartwell, my spiritual covering and friend. Thank you for your prayers of intercession, words of wisdom an example of manhood in the Kingdom. You are appreciated more than you will ever know.

Lastly, to Dr. T. L. Lowery, one of the greatest Spiritual giants and icons in history. Thank you for playing an extremely significant role in my life as a spiritual father and as a conduit of the power of God in the Earth. You have taught me more about the person of the Holy Spirit than I ever knew existed. You are truly missed on this side of

Heaven, but we know that you are resting in the arms of our Savior. I will see you on the other side Sir.

CONTENTS

Forward I by Mother Dorothy Norwood		*ix*
Forward II by Mayor Daniel Brown		*x*
Introduction		*2*
Chapter 1	The Person of the Holy Spirit	*8*
Chapter 2	Holy Spirit My Comforter	*18*
Chapter 3	Holy Spirit My Advocate	*26*
Chapter 4	Holy Spirit My Intercessor	*36*
Chapter 5	Holy Spirit My Counselor	*48*
Chapter 6	Holy Spirit My Strengthener	*58*
Chapter 7	Holy Spirit My Standby	*86*
Chapter 8	Holy Spirit My Teacher	*94*
Chapter 9	Holy Spirit My Reminder	*108*
Conclusion		*132*
Devotional		*137*
About the Author		*194*

FORWARD I

It is my honor to contribute to this awesome work of God written by my Spiritual son, Pastor Daryl Arnold. This book contains many scriptures and stories of the prophets of God. Each chapter will minister to any situation you experience in life - past, present, and future. It will lift your spirit, increase your faith, and bring joy to your soul. Allow yourself to be absorbed in this powerful and enlightening work as the Holy Spirit removes all doubt and brings you to a greater awareness of God and who He is in your life.

Mother Dorothy Norwood
Renown Gospel Artist

FORWARD II

It is indeed an honor and blessing to write the forward for this outstanding book by this great man of God. I have known Pastor Arnold for a number of years and have admired his work in the community and his leadership in the spiritual uplift in the city of Knoxville and beyond. He is a teacher, preacher, and family man who sets an example in Christian living for not only African-American men but for all to follow. I am sure this book will be an inspiration and encouragement for all who read it.

Daniel Brown
Former Mayor and City Councilman of Knoxville TN

hágios pneûma / Holy Spirit

"I have told you these things while I am still with you. But the Helper (Comforter, Advocate, Intercessor--Counselor, Strengthener, Standby), the Holy Spirit, whom the Father will send in My name [in My place, to represent Me and act on My behalf], He will teach you all things. And He will help you remember everything that I have told you."

John 14:25-26 AMP

INTRODUCTION

It was in the spring of 1992 at Knoxville College in Knoxville, TN. I was approaching the latter part of my collegiate career and was beginning to feel the pressure of trying to graduate in 5 years. I had enjoyed every aspect of the social life that comes with the college experience at an Historically Black College and University (HBCU). The fraternity, the parties, the popularity, and the ladies had pretty much made me forget that I was eventually supposed to graduate and live an adult life. I had at best a leftover religion from my early childhood and only really thought about God when I needed Him to raise my grade from a D to a C-. I think that I was saved but I definitely wasn't delivered. I had just enough Church experience in me to be able to have a decent debate with my Muslim friends who weren't really committed to their faith either.

One day I had an encounter with the Holy Spirit and not just an experience in Church. I was supposed to meet a close friend after his gospel choir rehearsal at the chapel. When I got there, they had not yet finished practicing so I decided just to sit on the back pew and wait until it was over. After a song or two, they began to sing a song that seemed to speak to everything that I was struggling with in life. It felt less like a song and more of a sermon that was being preached directly to me.

Pretty soon that song shifted from words, notes, and melodies to a tangible presence that began to overtake me. It was both awesome and awful at the same time. It was awesome because it was the first time that I had experienced the tangible presence of the Holy Ghost. But it was awful because I had never met Him before and it was scaring me. So, I did what any other college kid would do in that situation, I got up and I ran. Not in a figurative way but in a literal way. I literally took off running as fast and as far as I could to avoid this overwhelming presence. The only problem was that when I got up and ran, the Holy Spirit got up and ran with me. I know now that the Holy Spirit leads us into truth and righteousness but on this day, He wasn't leading me anywhere, He was literally chasing me! I mean physically chasing me down steep stairways, down narrow streets, and through parked cars. Chasing me between student housing facilities, through the science building, past the college center and even all the way to my dorm room. He even somehow managed to maneuver through a locked door. He was chasing me, and I was running out of gas.

I eventually found myself resting at the foot of my twin-sized bed and guess who was sitting right there beside me? Not only was this feeling real, but His presence was relentless. I found out that day that you will never be able to pursue the presence of the Spirit until you first have been pursued and arrested by Him.

I guess I'll never forget that day that I was chased and captured by the Holy Spirit on that small college campus, probably because it was the first effort of God to push me into my calling to preach. I wish I could say that I immediately began to walk with the Father but that wouldn't be true. There were many more games of “hide and go seek” that me and God had to play before

I completely surrendered. And if the truth be told, over two decades later, He still has to chase me around from time to time. I guess if you were to ask me what was the one memorable thing that I learned that day, it would be this, it wasn't enough for me to intellectually know God the Father as my creator and sustainer.

Therefore, my challenge to you in this book is to stop ignoring the precious gift of the Holy Spirit so that God would ignite a fire under your faith like never before. If you feel absent or void of the joy of your salvation, if you feel like there is something missing from your life in Christ, if you know that you're saved yet you still feel powerless over your sin, this book is perfect for you. This book will be the spark that will set your faith ablaze and will hopefully set others on fire in the same way. Journey with me as we walk through the Word of God and allow the Father to introduce you to another side of Himself in the person of the Holy Spirit. Let me, through the pages of this book, personally give you a formal introduction to the God in you.

CHAPTER 1
THE PERSON OF THE HOLY SPIRIT

The most important truth to acknowledge as we learn more about the Holy Spirit is that He is more than some intangible, invisible, unexplainable energy that stirs the emotions of Christians during a worship service, but the Holy Spirit is actually a real person and an equal partner of God Himself. You see, it's very difficult to develop a significant relationship or even fall in love with a mystical power that cannot be touched, experienced, or felt. When we paint a clear picture of the Holy Spirit as a person who desperately desires to be known and loved by humanity, then and only then can He be honored, cherished, and appreciated as He deserves to be.

Over the last year or so, I have been studying the African-American plight from the time that the first slave was taken from the sandy seashores of Africa up until our present day. As I read about the cruel and inhuman treatment of African slaves that were brought to the west against their will, it has both brought tears to my eyes and also raised questions in my head. Who in their right mind could kidnap people from their native lands, beat them beyond recognition, sell them like cheap property, hang them from oak trees in public places while receiving applause from onlookers? Who could be so mortally broken that they could walk away from a hanging corpse, go home, and have dinner with their families and then enjoy a good night's sleep? Even the most vile and evil soul would have difficulties doing that. How could it be so common without some sense of conviction or guilt? Well, I found the answer. The general population of that particular time did not see the slaves as human. They saw them as semi-intelligent animals or disposable property. Remember, up until almost the 1800's black people were legally only 3/5's human. That's why they could be treated poorly. They were not seen as people to build relationships with but property to simply be used.

This is a perfect illustration of how we as Believers have both viewed and treated the Holy Spirit. Because we have not seen Him to be a personality of God but have limited Him to simply being a piece of property from God, we have often times just used Him for our own personal benefits without intentionally developing a love relationship with Him. We see this played out in scripture in Acts 8 where Simon the Sorcerer was intrigued with the Apostle's ability to lay hands on the Believers so they would receive the gift of the Holy Spirit. He was so intrigued that he literally asked Peter could he purchase the Holy Spirit with money. He wanted to add the power of the Holy Spirit to his bag of tricks so that he could be an even bigger manipulator of people than he was before. Peter was so upset with the request that he openly cursed Simon and exiled him from the ministry. You see, although Simon had believed on God, he never saw the Holy Spirit as a person in God. He only saw Him as merely a possession from God.

Family, the Holy Spirit is so much more than an abstract object that God has given us to access His promises, but He is God Himself, worthy of the same honor, adoration, and reverence that we so easily give to God the Father and Jesus the Son. For they are all one and the same and deserve to be treated as such. Until we begin to recognize the Holy Spirit as a person, we will always neglect to receive the best out of our new life in Christ.

Follow me as we look to the scriptures that will consistently personify the Holy Spirit of God. Listen to what Jesus says about the Holy Spirit right before He is to be crucified. "I have told you these things while I am still with you. But the Helper (Comforter, Advocate, Intercessor--Counselor, Strengthener, Standby), the Holy Spirit, whom the Father will send in My name [in My place, to represent Me and act on My behalf], He will teach you all things. And He will help you remember everything that I have told you" (John 14:25-26 AMP).

Notice that all of the attributes of the Holy Spirit that are noted by Jesus are human characteristics. People are helpers to those that are helpless. People give comfort to the disheartened. People are advocates when others need assistance. People intercede for the voiceless. People give counsel to those that need wisdom. People give strength to those that are weak. People stand by one another in times of abandonment. Jesus intentionally uses these adjectives to let both the disciples of that day and the believers of this day know that the Holy Spirit should be perceived as a personality of God. He furthers the point by saying "He will teach you all things." Notice that He uses the Word "He." He is a personal pronoun that denotes the reality of one's human existence. Even Jesus Himself refuses to belittle the person of the Holy Spirit but He is determined to express their union equally. Look what He says to His disciples in John 14:26 AMP. He states, "When I depart, the Father will send you the Holy Spirit in My name [in My place, to represent Me and act on My behalf]." Jesus is very intentional about making it clear that He and the Spirit are one.

The challenge that I have for you is to begin to celebrate, appreciate, and honor the person of the Holy Spirit. When you speak of the Holy Spirit, train yourself to acknowledge Him not as an "IT" but as a personality of God. When you pray and acknowledge God the Father in your prayers and acknowledge Jesus your Savior in your prayers, also acknowledge the Holy Spirit. Just as an exercise, the next time you pray, start your prayer off by saying Holy Spirit, I thank you for your work in my life. Trust me it will be awkward because you typically will start your prayer off thanking the Father or either acknowledging Jesus. Try to discipline yourself to recognize the Holy Spirit for the true personality of God that He is.

He is more than our Holy God, but He is our Helping God. He is mentioned in John 14:25 as the Greek word, paráklēto. "One who is summoned, called to one's side, especially called to one's aid". Simply put, the Holy Spirit is one who comes alongside to help.

- *Parákl̄eto* is closely related to the word parachute. A parachute is what you depend upon when you are thousands of feet above the ground in an airplane and the plane malfunctions and is going down. You jump out the plane and pull your parachute and instead of falling to a horrible death you land safely on your feet. That's what the Holy Spirit does when the devil drops you from a high place in life and expects you to die. If you pull on the Holy Ghost, He will help you land on your feet.

- *Parákl̄eto* is closely related to the word paramedic. A paramedic is who you depend on when there has been an unexpected accident in your life. He's who you call when you need immediate care and assistance. That's what the Holy Spirit is to the Believer. When life has caught you off guard and you feel like you have wrecked your purpose and totaled your destiny you can call on the Holy Spirit and He will come to your rescue.

- *Parákl ēto* is where we get the word paralegal from. A paralegal is a type of lawyer that fights on your behalf even before you get in trouble. That's what the Holy Spirit does for us. He does not just advocate for us when we get ourselves in trouble, but He warns before we get in trouble. The Bible says that He is our very present help in times of trouble.

- *Paráklēto* is very closely related to the word periscope. A periscope is a tool that you use to see things that are present but can't be seen with the naked eye. That's what the Holy Spirit is to you, my friend. If you will use Him, He will help you to see things in the Spirit that you will never be able to see in the natural. That's why I'm writing this book because you need the Helper in your life! You need Him to help you when you feel helpless. He is not just our Holy God, but He is also our Helping God.

CHAPTER 2
HOLY SPIRIT MY COMFORTER

In this particular passage, Jesus first declares that the Holy Spirit will come to be our Comforter. In one of Jesus' first public sermons, He actually quotes Isaiah 61:1-3 NIV concerning the purpose of the Holy Spirit resting upon His life. "The Spirit of the Sovereign Lord is on me because the Lord has anointed me to proclaim good news to the poor. He has sent me to bind up the brokenhearted, to proclaim freedom for the captives and release from darkness for the prisoners, to proclaim the year of the Lord's favor and the day of vengeance of our God, to comfort all who mourn, and provide for those who grieve in Zion— to bestow on them a crown of beauty instead of ashes, the oil of joy instead of mourning, and a garment of praise instead of a spirit of despair. They will be called oaks of righteousness, a planting of the Lord for the display of his splendor."

The Spirit of God is truly the only one that can comfort us in our seasons of distress. I remember preaching the eulogy of not one but two baby siblings. It was the most difficult assignment that I have ever had in ministry. They had been trapped in the bedroom of a burning house and could not be rescued before they perished. I remember walking into the Church sanctuary and leading the family to view the babies for the final time. Because the family could not afford two caskets, they decided to bury both of the children in the same one. As I viewed the children, I broke down with emotion. A three-year-old little boy was holding his three-month-old little sister in a wooden box that was no more than 4 ft in length. What could I say to the family that would give any comfort at all in such a traumatic situation? The answer was nothing! With all of my homiletical skills, oratorical ability, and sermon prep, it just wasn't enough to soothe the pain of two lifeless babies in a small wooden box. The only hope that any of us had at that funeral was the comfort of the Holy Spirit. The Word promises us that He will bring comfort to all who mourn, and He will pour upon them that are grieving the oil of joy. I saw Him do it in the life of that family. I've seen Him do it in my own life over and over again and I can promise you that He will do the same for you in your time of distress. All you have to do is call upon Him. What you are dealing with right now might not be the loss of a child. Perhaps it's the loss of a marriage, the loss of a job, the loss of your health, the loss of a close relationship or even the loss of your dream but know that the Holy Spirit has oil for it all. He will heal you every place that you hurt. He will hold your hand as you walk through your valley of death and He will give you a peace that makes absolutely no scientific sense at all. I am a living witness family that not only will the Holy Spirit grieve with you, but He will grieve for you.

It's interesting that the Holy Spirit would call Himself a Comforter because the term is so relevant to the etymology of the Word. The Hebrew word for Spirit is RUACH which means wind or Breath. The Greek word for Spirit is the word Pneuma which renders the same definition, wind, and breath or life-giving source. The Holy Spirit is the power of God that gives us spiritual life. Genesis 2:7 NIV says "The Lord God formed a man from the dust of the ground and breathed into his nostrils the breath of life, and the man became a living being." When Man took his first breath in the natural it was an inhale. He literally inhaled the very life of God. When Man takes his last breath, it is an exhale. He surrenders that life back to God. This is also a process that must happen in the spirit realm in order for a man to be saved and have eternal life. You see when Adam sinned in the Garden of Eden the devil knocked the breath out of Adam. For God had already warned Adam that the day that he eats of the forbidden tree he would surely die. When Adam disobeyed God, it did not just knock the breath out of Adam but out of all creation that would come from the loins of Adam. Therefore, everyone born after Adam was delivered into the world stillborn. "Surely, I was sinful at birth, sinful from the time my mother conceived me. Yet you desired faithfulness even in the womb; you taught me wisdom in that secret place" (Psalm 51:5-6 NIV).

We were without God, without breath, and without life. But God loved us so much that He put His Holy lips on sinful people and breathed into us the Holy Spirit quickening us and giving us life. I used to call that spiritual CPR but that is a theological error. CPR is giving mouth to mouth resuscitation until a person can breathe on their own. God did not give us CPR because He knew that we could never breathe on our own without Him. So instead of giving us CPR, He does something better, He puts us on Eternal Life Support. Now that's a Comforter and that's something that I can find comfort in. I don't know about you, family, but I can't breathe without Him. I need Him every day, every hour and every moment of my life and I refuse to hold my breath. I refuse to allow the traditions of man and the lack of understanding about the Spirit of God to make me hold my breath. I pray that with every page that you read in this book that you would take a deeper breath. I pray that you will stay on the ventilator of His Spirit as you become more and more comfortable with the Comforter.

CHAPTER 3
HOLY SPIRIT MY ADVOCATE

Not only has the Holy Spirit promised that He would be our Comforter, but He has also promised to be our Advocate. The word advocate is defined as one who is to speak or write in favor of; support or urge by argument; recommend publicly. Romans 8:14-16 NIV says, "For those who are led by the Spirit of God are the children of God. The Spirit you received does not make you slaves so that you live in fear again; rather, the Spirit you received brought about your adoption to sonship. And by him, we cry, 'Abba,

Father.' The Spirit himself testifies with our spirit that we are God's children."

The context of this passage is centered around a group of Believers that had repented of their sins and had placed their confidence in Christ yet were still struggling internally with the questions of whether they really had obtained eternal life. They had allowed the traditions and expectations of others and the condemnation of self to pull them back under the bondage of the law. They thought that they had been saved by the grace of God, but they needed their own works of perfection to maintain their salvation. What a miserable way to live, to always live under the threat of losing your relationship with Christ based on self-justification. Paul encourages them by emphasizing that the Holy Spirit will never make them feel like slaves again. He wanted them to know that when they placed their faith in Christ that they had been forever set free. He strengthens His argument by stating that the Holy Spirit had acted as a lawyer or a witness on their behalf and had resolvedly won their case. He says that the Spirit testifies that we are the children of God. He creates this word picture of a person that is on trial waiting for a potential conviction. A conviction that could possibly render the consequences of an eternal death penalty.

However, just as the verdict is about to be stated, guilty as charged, God the Father calls two more witnesses to the stand, both Jesus and the Holy Spirit. Jesus testifies under oath that we truly are guilty of our sin and the devil had the evidence to prove it, but He also testified that although we were guilty He took on all of our sins upon the cross and paid the debt of the accused. 1 John 2:1 out of the NIV makes the point even the more salient, "My dear children, I write this to you so that you will not sin. But if anybody does sin, we have an advocate with the Father—Jesus Christ, the Righteous One."

Then the Holy Spirit takes the stand and testifies that Jesus really died for our sins and ultimately was raised from the grave as proof that the penalty was paid in full. However; we all know that the only time the witness' testimony can be deemed as credible is if the witness saw what he testifies of with his own eyes. The Holy Spirit is a credible eyewitness because the scripture says in Romans 8:11 that the Spirit Himself was the one that raised Jesus from the grave that we might be free. Therefore, there are two that bear witness that we have been declared righteous and we have no fear of separation from God, for in the presence of two witnesses a thing is established (2 Cor. 13:1).

Now here's the greatest part of the story. If you know anything about the judicial system you have heard of the phrase, double jeopardy. What that phrase means is that once a person has been tried and acquitted for a crime he or she can never be retried again and be convicted of the same crime. This means that we can now have total confidence in the finished work of the cross, for who the Son has set free is free indeed. You see, when we refuse to forgive ourselves for our shortcomings and resist the grace of God, it appears that our posture of unworthiness is a humble position. However, it is not. It is really a position of self-righteousness and pride. When we reject the free gift of forgiveness, we are saying to the Father that the death of His Son was not enough. We are saying to Him that the nails in His hands and feet were not sharp enough, the thorns upon His head were not deep enough, the spear through His side was not long enough, the grave that housed His body was not cold enough and the hell that He endured was not hot enough. What an insult to the God of our salvation when we dismiss His ultimate sacrifice and then guise it in humility. If you don't remember anything else that is written in this book remember this, your sin was not greater than His sacrifice. Confess your wrongs, repent to your Father, and get back up again. Never again allow the enemy to torture you with the lie that your God has abandoned you. Never again allow the nightmares of your past to keep you from enjoying the dreams of your future and never again lock yourself back into the prison cell of the law when God has given you the keys to His grace. Allow Jesus to be your Advocate with the Father and let the Holy Spirit be the Advocate to your own soul. May He constantly remind you of how you have been loved with an everlasting love.

Often times, I have been accused justifiably of ministering under assumption. What that means is taking for granted that the audience in which I'm speaking to has an in-depth understanding of the subject matter that I am speaking. However, this time I will not fall under that neglect. I have been writing about the Holy Spirit being our Advocate and our assurance that we have eternal life in Christ. The problem is that this everlasting life has only been reserved for the righteous and the only way that you can become righteous is for you to receive the free gift of His grace and forgiveness and I don't want to assume that you have received that gift. You could easily have this book about the Holy Spirit in your hand and not have the gift of the Holy Spirit in your heart.

Many years ago, I was preaching in Chattanooga, TN. As the service started a preacher introduced herself to me while we were sitting in the pulpit. She told me her name and then she started the worship service by leading the congregation in prayer. It was a great service. The choir was enthusiastic, the congregants were receptive, and I think that I preached a pretty good sermon.

After I got finished with the message, I gave the invitation to discipleship and simply challenged those that were without Christ to receive His love and forgiveness. I asked everyone who wasn't sure of their salvation to come down to the altar for prayer. Many came from the congregation to be saved. What was confusing is that the preacher who had sat next to me the entire service and had even prayed earlier went down too. I assumed that she was going to pray for others to be saved but little did I know; she had come down to be saved herself! How could this be, a woman in a black suit with a white clergy collar on her neck needed salvation? Yes exactly. Matthew 7:21-23 NIV clearly says, "Not everyone who says to me, 'Lord, Lord," will enter the Kingdom of heaven, but only the one who does the will of my Father who is in heaven. Many will say to me on that day, 'Lord, Lord, did we not prophesy in your name and in your name drive out demons and, in your name, perform many miracles?' Then I will tell them plainly, 'I never knew you. Away from me, you evildoers!'" That night I realized that you can have a reserved seat in the pulpit in Church but not have a reserved seat in Heaven. I realized that although her name was written in the Church bulletin it did not mean her name had been written in the Lamb's book of life. So, I have never ministered under assumption since that night and I refuse to do it today.

Maybe you are reading this book and you don't know Christ. You don't know what would happen to you if your heart stopped beating right now. Today I have some good news. You don't have to wait until you go to some Church on Sunday. You don't have to wait for some preacher to shake your hand and pray for you. And the best news is that you don't have to wait to get your life right to come to Jesus. You can come to Him just as you are and just where you are. If you pray this prayer now in the comfort of your home or wherever you are, He will save you immediately. He will wash away your sins forever and your past will be forgotten. Please pray this prayer with me:

Say, "Father in Jesus' name. I thank you for giving me the opportunity to hear the Gospel explained in this book. I believe by faith that you sent your Son Jesus to die for me and to forgive me for all of my sins. I believe that He died on a cross for me, He went to hell for me and rose again that I may receive eternal life. Please come into my heart so that I might live the rest of my life for You. I am saved in Jesus' name. Amen." If you prayed that prayer and you meant it, the Holy Spirit just moved into your heart and is advocating on your behalf. Your past has been erased, your present is being established and I look forward to your future. Welcome to the Kingdom of God!

CHAPTER 4
HOLY SPIRIT MY INTERCESSOR

Prayer is one of the most significant spiritual disciplines of the Christian faith. It is the gift that God has given us to both have consistent union with Him and also to receive the knowledge we need to fulfill our assignment here on Earth. Nothing happens on the Earth in public for the Believer without prayers going up in private from the Believer. Jesus Himself had to depend upon the discipline of prayer in order for Him to be effective on the Earth. He said in John 5:19, "I only do what I see the Father do." He was talking about how He was constantly connecting to the

Father in prayer to determine what His assignment would be for that day. Have you ever noticed the pattern of how Jesus would heal the sick, cleanse the lepers, give sight to the blind and even raise the dead yet would never be unsuccessful at any of them? Have you ever thought about how He could always bat 100 in ministry without fail? I personally don't think that His success was based upon some cookie cutter ministry strategy that He read in a book or gleaned from a leadership conference. I think it was based upon His discipline in the morning.

Every day, even before the disciples would wake up, Jesus was either on a mountain or in a garden somewhere praying. It was so typical of Him that even when Judas wanted to betray Jesus he knew exactly where He could be found, in the Garden of Gethsemane, the place of prayer. I believe that the miracles we see Him work in the scriptures were merely the harvest of the prayer seeds that were constantly sown throughout His ministry. If you would ever take advantage of the gift of prayer it would relieve you of unnecessary weight that you were never designed to carry. It would give you divine insight into the will of God and it would make you so much more effective in accomplishing your God-given goals. There are certain things that you will never see with your eyes that you have not first spoken of out of your mouth. Prayer really does make the difference.

A few years ago, we purchased our first ministry facility. One of the rooms in the building that I was looking forward to equipping was the workout facility. I remember purchasing three treadmills from a local sports store and transporting them to the Church. I was about to take one of them off of the truck when one of my deacons challenged me to leave it there. He said, Pastor, you stick to preaching and leave the heavy lifting to the professionals. When I heard that of course, I had to prove a point. I grabbed one of the treadmills by the handles and lifted it up like I was Superman. The only problem was that my back reminded me that I was really Clark Kent. I pulled a muscle that was so painful that I couldn't even stand up straight. The pain was excruciating. I quickly dropped the treadmill and called a Chiropractor that was a member of my Church. He found out that I had popped a rib out of place but because of his training he was able to pop it right back into its proper position. I looked at him and said well, I guess I won't be lifting anything else heavy. He replied, Pastor it's ok for you to lift heavy items you just have to learn how to lift them the right way. He said that you've been trying to lift the weight with your back instead of using your knees. He said that my back was never designed to bear weight, that's what my knees were made for.

Right then God spoke to me. He said that this was not just true about lifting weight in the natural but also the spiritual. We often try to carry weight in our lives that we were never designed to carry. We try to lift the burdens and problems that are far too heavy for us and we consequently find ourselves bent over emotionally in pain and frustration. When God has told us over and over again to come to Him in prayer and He would carry our weight. He tells us to use our knees in prayer and He will in turn lift our heavy loads.

When Jesus said to come to Him all of us who are heavy laden and He would give us rest, He is saying use your knees. When the Father says to cast our cares on Him for He cares for us, He is saying use your knees. When the Master challenges us to take no thought for what we will eat, or drink, or wear but to seek Him first, He is saying use your knees. When Paul tells us to be anxious for nothing but in all things pray and

God will give us peace that passes all understanding, He is telling us to use our knees. Stop trying to fix what's broken, mend what's torn, fill what's empty and lift what's heavy in your own fleshly abilities. It only leads you to a broken and bent over spirit. Use your knees and give it to God in prayer, He will carry your load. "Lift up your eyes and look to the heavens: Who created all these? He who brings out the starry host one by one and calls forth each of them by name. Because of his great power and mighty strength, not one of them is missing. Why do you complain, Jacob? Why do you say, Israel, 'My way is hidden from the Lord; my cause is disregarded by my God?' Do you not know? Have you not heard? The Lord is the everlasting God, the Creator of the ends of the Earth. He will not grow tired or weary, and his understanding no one can fathom. He gives strength to the weary and increases the power of the weak. Even youths grow tired and weary, and young men stumble and fall, but those who hope in the Lord will renew their strength. They will soar on wings like eagles; they will run and not grow weary; they will walk and not be faint" (Isaiah 40:26-31 NIV).

But let's just be honest sometimes we don't go to our knees because the load is so severe that we just don't know what to pray for. Have you ever been in so much pain or just so emotionally overwhelmed in life that you wanted to pray, you just couldn't figure out where to start or even what to say? Those are the times that you need an intercessor. Those are the times that you need someone to assist you in your petitions to the Lord and even stand in the gap and pray for you. Just the other day my son was in so much pain that all he could do was cry in agony. Every time that I would ask him what was hurting him, he could only respond with an inaudible cry. His little brother had to eventually tell me that He was dealing with a migraine headache. You see sometimes you can be under so much pressure in life that you can't speak to the Father on your own. You need someone to talk to Him on your behalf. That's called INTERCESSION my friend and everybody will eventually need an intercessor. The Apostle Paul addresses this very thing in Roman 8:26-28 as he tries to encourage the Believers at the Church of Rome. Let me share it out of the Message Bible for clarity. He says, "Meanwhile, the moment we get tired in the waiting, God's Spirit is right alongside helping us along. If we don't know how or what to pray, it doesn't matter. He does our praying in and for us, making prayer out of our wordless sighs, our aching groans. He knows us far better than we know ourselves, knows our pregnant condition, and keeps us present before God. That's why we can be so sure that every detail in our lives of love for God is worked into something good."

Can you hear the voice of care and concern coming from the Holy Spirit in the tone of this text? Doesn't this sound like a confidant or a friend rather than an intangible ball of energy that periodically shows up at Church from time to time? Verse 26 says that the Holy Spirit helps us when we get tired. That word "help" there literally means to share a heavy load. Just as the example that was given earlier concerning the treadmill. When we get tired and weighed down with the cares of this world the Holy Spirit shares the load and prays with us. But not only that, when we have no idea what to pray, He begins to pray for us. Wow, how amazing is that to know that when you can't pray for yourself and when others are too busy to pray for you the Holy Spirit Himself is praying inside of you? That takes all of the stress and expectations off of you when you're not sure if others are interceding for you or not. As a Pastor, I often hear people voice their grievances that they don't have anyone to consistently pray with them or for them. My response is always this. Know that even when everyone else has neglected to pray for you, you yet always have two people that never stop praying on your behalf. Jesus is at this very moment at the right-hand side of the Father making intercession for you and the Holy Spirit is making intercession within you, and trust me, those two definitely know how to get a prayer through.

When my wife was pregnant with our first daughter, she didn't get a lot of sleep. She was trying to adjust to nausea in the mornings, the uncomfortable positioning of the baby during the day and the abrupt twist and turns of the baby at night. I would sleep close to her at night to try to bring as much comfort as I could. One night while I was sleeping, I noticed that my wife every 5 or 10 minutes would wake me up with a sharp nudge to my side. I would wake her up and ask her what she wanted, and she would say that she did not nudge me at all. This happened four or five times straight, interrupting my rest all night. The last time I pretended to be asleep to see if she would do it again. Just as I had expected about 5 minutes later, she nudged me on my side again but then I realized something interesting. Her hands were not touching me at all, and she was sound asleep. It was the baby that was inside of her that had been kicking me all night. You see although she was fast asleep and unconscious to the world, the thing that was inside of her was wide awake trying to communicate with me. Sometimes we are so tired in life that we are unconscious to prayer. We don't know what to say and don't know how to say it, but just like my daughter was wide awake inside her sleeping mother so is the Holy Spirit wide awake in us interceding on our behalf. He's praying for your health when you are sick. He's praying for your finances when you are short. He's praying for your family when your home is in shambles. He's praying for your marriage when it's falling apart and He's praying for your mind when you have need of direction. When you feel like you have nothing to say to God, nothing to give to God or nothing to receive from God, know that the Holy Spirit is praying inside you.

CHAPTER 5
HOLY SPIRIT MY COUNSELOR

I am a counselor by assumption. Most people just automatically assume that their Pastor or spiritual leader is qualified to speak into their lives from a professional perspective. However, in most cases that is not true at all. Most of us are only equipped to speak into a person's life from a Biblical perspective. However, the benefit of the ministry that God gave me is that He has blessed me with the gift of Biblical insight, and He has also given my wife the gift of professional insight. She is an authentic counselor by both trade and training. Therefore, I thought that it would probably be wise to ask her what her working definition of a counselor was and how does one benefit most effectively from their expertise.

What she said was critical to writing this chapter. This was her response, "Someone trained to provide wisdom, guidance, and support through life's issues and challenges. One can benefit the most from a counselor if they commit to being honest about their own personal deficits and areas that they want to improve coupled with being open to the idea of pushing past challenging experiences to gain greater insight and understanding." I guess the bottom line is that a counselor is a person that you willfully give permission to help influence your decision-making process.

The Bible likens the Holy Spirit as a counselor. This means that the only way that we can fully benefit from and get the best out of His counsel is to willfully give Him permission to help shape and influence our decisions. I am convinced that that is why so many people and religious institutions continue to ignore the Holy Spirit and keep Him on the periphery of their lives. They don't want Him to be in control because losing control of anything is scary. So, we settle for having the Spirit around us in our preaching, our devotions, as logos on t-shirts and in our worship music instead of being filled with Him in our hearts. Even hearing the phrase, "FILLED WITH THE HOLY SPIRIT," made many of you nervous while reading this book. Let me first be extremely clear theologically. I am not saying that you don't have the Holy Spirit living inside of you. The Bible is very clear that if you have not the Holy Spirit you don't even belong to Christ.

The Holy Spirit is the seal of our salvation and the birthmark of every Believer. However, I am saying that you can have the Holy Spirit living within in you but now allow Him to be actively working in you, on you and for you. Although every true Christian is in possession of the Holy Spirit, the Father is yet still challenging us all to desire more and more of Him on a daily basis. The Bible says in Ephesians 5:18-20, "Do not get drunk on wine, which leads to debauchery. Instead, be filled with the Spirit, speaking to one another with psalms, hymns, and songs from the Spirit. Sing and make music from your heart to the Lord, always giving thanks to God the Father for everything, in the name of our Lord Jesus Christ."

Many people have used this passage as a Biblical argument to condemn Believers who drink alcohol. I have my own personal beliefs in regard to drinking and Christianity but regardless of what those beliefs are they couldn't be validated or invalidated by using this passage. These verses have absolutely nothing to do with whether a

Believer should drink or not. This passage is contextually about how the Holy Spirit is designed to influence a person's life. The mention of not being filled with wine is an allegory that Paul is trying to use to get the readers to understand the power of the Holy Spirit when one gets filled with Him. Just as being filled with wine influences your life so does being filled with the Spirit. Let's just think about this for a moment. What happens to a person when they keep filling themselves with alcoholic beverages? It first changes their walk. When you are filled with the Holy Spirit, He will change your walk for the steps of a good man will be ordered by the Lord. Being filled with alcohol will then change the way you talk. So will being filled with the Spirit. You will begin to confess the Word of God and speak blessings over the lives of others. Being filled with alcohol will also change your thinking. Drunk people often have confidence while drunk that they don't have when they are sober. When we are filled with the Spirit, we will begin to walk in the Kingdom confidence of God and will ultimately walk by Faith and not by fear.

This illustration is not a theological stretch at all. We have seen the same word picture in Acts 2 when the Holy Spirit fell for the first time on the Church. It was with such power that many believed that those that were filled with the Spirit were drunk. Just as drinking alcohol controls the consumer, so will being filled with the Spirit control the Believer. The problem is that if you stop consuming the Spirit, you will eventually sober up, just as you would with alcohol. That's why God challenges us not to simply be filled once with the Holy Spirit, but He wants us to keep on drinking so that He can continue to influence our decisions. Now here's the blessing, you don't have to pay for it. Drinks are on the house. All you have to do is avail yourself to the fountain of God and He will fill you with His new wine.

The Holy Spirit our Counselor also leads the Believer. Romans 8:14 NIV says "For those who are led by the Spirit of God are the children of God." John 16:13 NIV says, "But when he, the Spirit of truth, comes, he will guide you into all the truth. He will not speak on his own; he will speak only what he hears, and he will tell you what is yet to come."

Galatians 5:18 NIV says, but if you are led by the Spirit, you are not under the Law. You see the Holy Spirit leads and guides us. God has given every one of His children a Spiritual GPS to navigate through this life. However, no GPS works if the owner of the vehicle refuses to activate it. Now is the time to turn the Holy Spirit on in your life. He will lead you into your next major assignment. He will order every step and make every path clear if you don't refuse to ignore His existence. Allow Him to lead you even if the path becomes dark and unfamiliar, He knows what's best for you.

In Matthew 4:1-2 NIV, "Jesus was led by the Spirit into the wilderness to be tempted by the devil. After fasting forty days and forty nights, he was hungry." You see every time the Spirit leads you it's not into green pastures, sometimes He leads you into dark wilderness. But wherever He leads you to, know that there is a purpose and that He will bring you out better than you were before you went in. Matthew 4 says that Jesus was led into the wilderness to be tempted by the devil but don't forget that the chapter before Jesus was filled with the Holy Spirit by His Father in Heaven. "As soon as Jesus was baptized, he went up out of the water. At that moment heaven was opened, and he saw the Spirit of God descending like a dove and alighting on him. And a voice from heaven said, 'This is my Son, whom I love; with Him I am well pleased'" (Matthew 3:16-17 NIV).

If you are filled with the Spirit, it doesn't matter what environment you find yourself in. You can be living in a mansion on a hill or living in a cardboard box on the street. You can be resting in a king size bed or in an ICU hospital bed. You can be vacationing on a cruise ship or locked behind prison bars. He will protect you from it all and He will give you joy in the midst of your sorrow.

There's a song that our worship team used to sing when I was doing campus ministry for Intervarsity Christian Fellowship that has always stuck with me. It was called Breathe on Me[1]. The lyrics were: "Breathe on me, Breathe on me. Holy

[1] Clint Brown. 2009. "Breathe on Me." *In His Presence,* compact disc. Genre: Christian/Gospel.

Ghost power Breathe on me. Yesterday is gone today I'm in need. Holy Ghost power Breathe on me." The lyrics of that song have gotten me through some of the most difficult times of my life. The song is basically asking the Holy Spirit to fill us with His presence over and over again. It is saying that yesterday's encounter has expired and is no longer sufficient for the new day that is approaching. It is challenging us not to become comfortable and content with what the Holy Spirit has done in our lives in the past but continue to seek Him and depend upon Him for new experiences in the future.

CHAPTER 6
HOLY SPIRIT MY STRENGTHENER

February of 2017 was one of the most frightening times of my life. I had been preaching in Houston, TX and was boarding my plane to come back home to Knoxville. I fell asleep on the plane just as I always do and was awakened to a slight headache behind my right eye. It wasn't really painful just a bit aggravating. I arrived home, greeted my family and decided to go to bed early to sleep it off. About 4:00 a.m. the next morning I woke up with the same pain behind my eye except for this time I also felt like I had pressure building up on the right side of my head.

I went into the bathroom to get some medicine and realized that I couldn't blink. Immediately I begin to look into the mirror to see what was going on. Not only could I not blink but I had lost all of the muscle control on that side of my face. By the time that I made it to the hospital my entire face on that side had fallen, I had lost the ability to smell out of my right nostril and my speech had started to slur. Everyone at the hospital including me was assuming that I was having a stroke. However, when all of the test results came back, we found out that it wasn't a stroke, but something called Bell's palsy. It's a type of facial paralysis that resembles a stroke.

Bell's palsy is the result of a single nerve failure that sits deep inside the inner ear that controls the entire muscle function in the face. If that single nerve malfunctions and stops working properly it will affect the entire mobility of one's face. It was so difficult to believe that something so obscure and seemingly unimportant could control so much of the body. This is a perfect parallel with the Holy Spirit. It is amazing how the Holy Spirit could be so overlooked and underappreciated. Yet He controls so much of the Body of Christ. Just as the nerve in the inner ear brings strength to your face, the Holy Spirit is what gives strength to our lives. He cannot be seen; many times, can't be felt and sits in the most inner part of our bodies. Yet if He stops working in and on us, we will undoubtedly lose our strength.

In Acts 1:6-8, Jesus' disciples gathered around Him and asked him, "Lord, are you at this time going to restore the Kingdom to Israel?" He said to them: "It is not for you to know the times or dates the Father has set by his own authority. But you will receive POWER when the Holy Spirit comes on you." Jesus had given His disciples the assignment to do what He did in the Earth while He was gone. He charged them to heal the sick, preach the Kingdom and set the captive free but He knew that they would not be able to do it unless they used the same power that He used, the Power of the Holy Ghost. Although God took the Body of Jesus up to be with Him in Heaven, He sent the Spirit of Jesus down to be with us on Earth. There are too many of us that are trying to fulfill the purpose of God without using the power of God. If Jesus was completely dependent upon the Power of the Holy Spirit to accomplish His Kingdom endeavors, we probably are going to have to be dependent upon the Holy Spirit to accomplish ours.

The Power to Become Witnesses

The Holy Spirit first gives us the power to witness. "Then they gathered around him and asked him, 'Lord, are you at this time going to restore the Kingdom to Israel?' He said to them: 'It is not for you to know the times or dates the

Father has set by his own authority. But you will receive power when the Holy Spirit comes on you, and you will be my witnesses in Jerusalem, and in all Judea and Samaria, and to the ends of the Earth"' (Acts 1:6-8 NIV). Generally, when you think of the Holy Spirit you don't immediately associate it with evangelism, but Jesus does. He understands that if we need power for anything it's the power to witness. You see if you really look to the scriptures concerning what Jesus' primary pursuits were, you will discover something extremely interesting. Jesus only came looking for two things. The Bible says that He came looking for worshippers and to seek and to save the lost. What's so sad is that everybody says that they are followers of Christ, but nobody wants to truly worship or to seek the lost. As a matter of fact, according to many current surveys concerning Christianity, only 15% of all Believers have ever shared the Gospel with anyone in their entire lives. Most people leave that up to the preacher and deacon, but Jesus clearly left a mandate to all Believers to witness.

The closest that most people get to share the Gospel is to invite someone to come to Church with them. I'm definitely not against inviting people to Church but the Great Commission never was about compelling people to come to Church but to compel people to come into the Kingdom of God. One of my mentors used to tell me that she believes that when we go to Heaven that God would ask us two questions, who did we love and who did we bring with us? I wonder if we refuse to bring people with us, did we really love them at all. This is the time when many people will close this book and never pick it back up again because it's becoming more and more convicting to the soul. I've come to realize that most people love revelation from God but hate being responsible to God. But if you'll keep this book open and resist the temptation to check out and surf the pages of your social media accounts, I promise that you will be a better witness for Jesus when you're done.

Actually, most people have very valid reasons why they don't share the Gospel. The first one is that they don't think people will listen. This could not be any further from the truth. Jesus said it best in Matthew 9. He said that the Harvest was plentiful. It's the laborers that were few. What He was saying is that there's a great harvest of souls that He has prepared to come into His Kingdom, but He doesn't have enough Believers to go gather them. He is saying through farming terminology that people are dying on the vine and going to hell because Christians would not get over their fear of rejection and complacency. That's why you need the power of the Holy Spirit to overcome your fear of rejection.

The second reason that many people say that they fear witnessing is that they don't think that they are knowledgeable enough about the Bible. I mean what if I witness and I'm challenged on scripture? How will I respond if I'm asked a Biblical question and don't know the answer? Remember, God never called you to know Hebrew, Greek or Arabic. He never asked you to be theologically weighty or doctrinally deep. He never said that you had to have a seminary degree or Doctor of Theology. He called you to be a witness and the only responsibility of a witness is to testify of what you have experienced. Testify of how He brought you out of darkness into the marvelous light. Testify to how He broke addictions off of your life that was unbreakable before you met Him. Testify of how He has filled the voids in your life and has given you peace unspeakable. Just giving testimony of His love in your life is enough to draw sinners to the saving knowledge of Christ. Listen to the words of Paul as He deals with the same fear of inadequacy that we often have in regard to evangelism. "And so, it was with me, brothers and sisters. When I came to you, I did not come with eloquence or human wisdom as I proclaimed to you the testimony about God. For I resolved to know nothing while I was with you except Jesus Christ and him crucified. I came to you in weakness with great fear and trembling. My message and my preaching were not with wise and persuasive words, but with a demonstration of the Spirit's power so that your faith might not rest on human wisdom, but on God's power" (1 Corinthians 2:1-5 NIV).

Power to Become Warriors

I'm not sure if you recognize it or not but if you're saved, you're in the middle of a fight. Just because you have 5000 Facebook friends and a million Instagram followers that does not mean that everyone is in love with you. Trust me the devil hates you and his mission is to kill, steal and destroy everything that you desire to accomplish. One of the devil's greatest tricks is to make us believe that our lives are limited to what we can see with the naked eye. He wants to have us so focused on our families, our friends, our finances, and our future that we lose sight of the reality that we are in a spiritual fight! Jesus said that the Kingdom of God suffers violence but the violent takes it by force.

2 Timothy 4:6-7 NIV says, "For I am already being poured out like a drink offering, and the time for my departure is near. I have fought the good fight, I have finished the race, I have kept the faith."

Ephesians 6:10-17 NIV says, "Finally, be strong in the Lord and in his mighty power. Put on the full armor of God, so that you can take your stand against the devil's schemes. For our struggle is not against flesh and blood, but against the rulers, against the authorities, against the powers of this dark world and against the spiritual forces of evil in the heavenly realms. Therefore, put on the full armor of God, so that when the day of evil comes, you may be able to stand your ground, and after you have done everything, to stand. Stand firm then, with the belt of truth buckled around your waist, with the breastplate of righteousness in place, and with your feet fitted with the readiness that comes from the gospel of peace. In addition to all this, take up the shield of faith, with which you can extinguish all the flaming arrows of the evil one. Take the helmet of salvation and the sword of the Spirit, which is the word of God."

Paul challenges us to put our armor on every day because the very day that you decide not to put it on will be the day when the enemy will attack you the hardest. He says to put your belt of truth on because if not the devil will infiltrate your soul with lies. He says to put on the breastplate of righteousness because he will try to poison your heart with unrighteousness. He says to guard your feet with the gospel of peace so that he can't convince you to walk down the path of confusion. He tells us to pick up the shield of faith, so the devil can't penetrate our hearts with fear. He tells us to put on the helmet of salvation, so he can't manipulate our thoughts and play tricks on our minds. Finally, He tells us to pick up the Sword of the Spirit which is the Word of God so that we can cut the head off of the devil just as David cut the head off of Goliath. But none of this can happen without using the weapon of mass destruction that the Father has given us, the Holy Spirit!

Whether you want to accept it or not, my friend you have been drafted into a spiritual war and you need the power and the strength of the Holy Spirit to win. In Ezekiel 37, the Bible tells of a story of God placing the Prophet Ezekiel in a valley full of dry bones. He asked the prophet a question: Can these bones live again? Then God gives him the strategy of how to resurrect the dead bodies that are in front of him. The first thing He tells him to do is to prophesy or speak life into the bones. After Ezekiel did it the Bible says the bones came together one by one and piece by piece. Then the Lord caused muscle, ligaments, and skin to cover the bones. There was only one problem. Because there was no breath in them, they yet remained dead. The Lord then told Ezekiel to prophesy or pray to the wind which is the Holy Spirit. Did you hear that? God told Ezekiel to pray to the Holy Spirit! How many times have you actually done that?

In response to his prayer, the Spirit entered each body and they stood up as a mighty army. Notice that they only stood up as warriors after the Spirit entered them and so it is with us. God has called us to come together and war against the powers of darkness. He called us to war against injustice in our communities. He's called us to war against turmoil in our families. He's called us to war against the unrighteousness in our world. Many times, I hear people complain about how the devil is attacking their lives. I'm not being insensitive when I say this because he's attacking mine too but instead of complaining about the devil's attacks, how about deciding to fight back!

We can't continue to allow the enemy to just create havoc in our lives and not use the weapons that God gave us to retaliate. I was taught as a little boy that the moment you decide to stand up to the bully, the bully stops bullying you and tries to make friends. We've got to fight back with our faith, but we cannot be effective and successful as warriors for Christ until we are filled with the power of His Spirit. When we walk in the truth, we can be confident of this one thing, "It's not by might nor by power, but by my Spirit, says the Lord Almighty" (Zechariah 4:3,6 NIV).

Power Over Our Weakness

I had a friend once that debated with me for almost an hour that a person was not truly saved if they did not speak in tongues. His argument was based upon the belief that tongues were the ultimate sign of being filled with the Holy Spirit. Don't get me wrong, I do believe that all of the gifts of the Spirit are still alive and active today just as they were in the past. I personally have a prayer language and have walked with many others as they have sought the gift. However, I do not believe that speaking in tongues is a prerequisite to salvation nor is it the only proof of a person being filled with the Holy Spirit. As a matter of fact, the primary purpose of the Holy Spirit is in the etymology of the word itself. He's called the Holy Spirit, which is the Spirit of Holiness. He's not called the spirit of tongue, or prophecy, or miracles or interpretation. He's called the Spirit of Holiness because that's how He desires to work in our lives, to help us live Holy. I know people who speak in tongues but won't speak to their own spouse after a disagreement. I know people who can prophetically see the faults of others but can never see their own personal flaws. I know people who tarry with strangers for hours in hopes that they will be filled with the Holy Spirit but won't take 20 minutes out of their day to help their own child with their homework. I know people who fall down backward on the floor when the preacher lays his hands on them but have absolutely no intentions at all to live for Christ when they get up. The Holy Spirit is not just obligated to express His power on the outside of man but to help the weaknesses that are hidden within the inside of man.

You are aware that all of us have weaknesses. Every one of you, reading this book is struggling with a weakness that you have been wrestling with for years. Whether you are a 90-year-old Bishop or a 9-year-old kid, we all have a weakness. The things that keep you up all night. The thing that keeps you on your face at the altar. The thing that most of us hope to God is never revealed or exposed publicly. It's the constant internal yearning of your flesh that is unlike God that the enemy is always tempting you with. This universal truth should humble all of us and hopefully keep us from becoming judgmental of others when their weaknesses are exposed. You see being JUDGMENTAL is being the JUDGE of others in your own MIND. It's the arrogance of thinking that your weakness is not as big as the weakness of others. The Apostle James puts it this way in the Message Bible, "Don't let anyone under pressure to give in to evil say, 'God is trying to trip me up.' God is impervious to evil and puts evil in no one's way. The temptation to give in to evil comes from us and only us. We have no one to blame but the leering, seducing flare-up of our own lust. Lust gets pregnant and has a baby: sin! Sin grows up to adulthood and becomes a real killer" (James 1:13-15 MSG).

One day I was at a relative's home for dinner and they had boiled okra on the menu. Yuuuuuuck, who in their right mind would eat that nasty stuff. As I sat and watched my uncle devour one helping after another of that disgusting bowl of green slime, I almost got sick at my stomach. Why would he have such an appetite for something so gross? I criticized him with every bite. The next day I came home, and my mother had cooked dinner and guess what was on the menu, okra. However, this time it was not boiled and slimy, it was fried and crispy and if anybody knows me, I cannot resist a big bowl of fried crispy okra. As I took the first bite, I was quickly convicted. You see the same thing that I had condemned my uncle for liking on the day before, I had a weakness for the next day. It was still okra it was just presented differently. All of us have an appetite for some kind of sin and the devil sure does know how to cook it up to appeal to your particular appetite. That's why we should never criticize and condemn others for their weakness because we have one of our own. Instead of condemning, we need to be calling on the Holy Ghost to help us with them and I promise you, He has the desire and the ability to do just that. Romans 8:11 NIV says, "And if the Spirit of him who raised Jesus from the dead is living in you, he who raised Christ from the dead will also give life to your mortal bodies because of his Spirit who lives in you." This text should excite you to know that there is no sin that has its grip on you that the Holy Spirit is not able to break. But it should also invite you to the altar of God to ask Him to help strengthen you in your areas of weakness. You do not have the responsibility or the power to clean yourself up, but you do have a responsibility to submit yourself to the power of the Holy Spirit.

Have you ever gone through one of those automatic car washes where you don't get out of your car while it's being washed? I went through one just the other day. It had been raining in Knoxville for about 3 weeks straight and every car on the road was covered with dirt and mud. When the sun finally came out, I decided to go get my car washed. I pulled up to the wash bay and there was a man outside giving instructions on how it all worked. He pointed at a sign that had very important directives. Put your car in neutral. Take your foot off the brake and take your hands off of the steering wheel. I hate those car washes because when you go through them you don't have any control over your vehicle. That's probably the same reason that I struggle with the work of the Holy Spirit in my life. I don't like yielding my life completely to Him and losing control. Don't judge me, you don't like to totally lose control either. However, if we don't put our lives in neutral and allow God to order our steps, if we don't take our foot off of the brake and trust Jesus to push us forward and if we don't take our hands off the steering wheel and allow the Master to guide us, we will never come out on the other side clean before God. I went into the carwash covered with dirt and mud but when I surrendered to the process and enjoyed the journey, I came out completely clean without any human effort of my own. I thank God daily that He has not just saved me by His grace, but He has also sanctified me with His Spirit. In the words of one of the most flawed yet favored characters in the Bible, King David, "Create in me a pure heart, O God, and renew a steadfast spirit within me. Do not cast me from your presence or take your Holy Spirit from me. Restore to me the joy of your salvation and grant me a willing spirit, to sustain me. Then I will teach transgressors your ways so that sinners will turn back to you" (Psalm 51:10-13 NIV).

Power To Become Worshippers

"Yet a time is coming and has now come when the true worshipers will worship the Father in the Spirit and in truth, for they are the kind of worshipers the Father seeks. God is Spirit, and his worshipers must worship in the Spirit and in truth" (John 4:23-24 NIV).

In this passage, Jesus makes it clear that the act of worship is much more than a choir or worship team leading a congregation in a couple of songs and staying on key. He declared that worship is a spiritual act. Something that must be initiated and maintained by the Spirit of God. Many times, we have reduced worship to an act of traditional foreplay before the preacher starts His sermon. We often place more emphasis on the pitch of the song rather than the power of the Spirit. If we would ever realize the power of real spirit-led worship, it would change our entire lives.

I don't want to bore you with so much scripture here, but I think that it is necessary for you to understand the significance of God-driven worship. Listen to this story in 1 Samuel. "Now the Spirit of the Lord had departed from Saul, and an evil spirit from the Lord tormented him. Saul's attendants said to him, 'See, an evil spirit from God is tormenting you. Let our lord command his servants here to search for someone who can play the lyre. He will play when the evil spirit from God comes on you, and you will feel better.' Saul said to his attendants, 'Find someone who plays well and bring him to me.' One of the servants answered, 'I have seen a son of Jesse of Bethlehem who knows how to play the lyre. He is a brave man and a warrior. He speaks well and is a fine-looking man. And the Lord is with him.' Then Saul sent messengers to Jesse and said, 'Send me your son David, who is with the sheep.' So, Jesse took a donkey loaded with bread, a skin of wine and a young goat and sent them with his son David to Saul. David came to Saul and entered his service. Saul liked him very much, and David became one of his armor- bearers. Then Saul sent word to Jesse, saying, 'Allow David to remain in my service, for I am pleased with him.' Whenever the spirit from God came on Saul, David would take up his lyre and play. Then relief would come to Saul; he would feel better, and the evil spirit would leave him" (1 Samuel 16:14-23 NIV).

There are a couple of powerful principles that I think are noteworthy from the passage. First, when the story opens up with, the Spirit of the Lord had departed from Saul, and an evil spirit from the Lord tormented him, it's not saying God sent evil to torment Saul because God has no evil in Him. But it is saying that whenever you get out of the will of God and you lose His presence you are vulnerable to the attacks of the enemy. Where the Spirit of the Lord is, there is liberty but where the Spirit of the Lord ain't there is bondage, and I did mean to say "ain't" to express the seriousness of the point. It is dangerous to rebel against the will of God because you not only lose His presence, but you also lose His protection.

The second point to be noted is that Saul was struggling with some sort of depression or anxiety that he could not escape. He tried everything that he could but to no avail. Saul's servant then came up with a brilliant suggestion. Let's get David who is a skilled musician to play his harp for you and maybe the depression will release you. He called for David and David played for him. Immediately the atmosphere changes and the evil spirits left the room.

The key was not that David was a skilled musician. The key was that the Lord's Spirit was upon David and He used it to change the atmosphere. That's what true worship in the Spirit is supposed to do. Change the atmosphere with such an impact that depression, worry, and anxiety leaves you while you're in worship. I have a challenge for those of you who are ministry leaders. Don't hire a band or worship leader predicated upon their musical talents. Hire them based upon their ability to use the Spirit of God to change the atmosphere. I challenge all musicians and singers who are reading this book to spend less time perfecting your musical craft and spend more time bathing in the Spirit of God. It takes a change of atmosphere in worship to destroy yokes and remove burdens and not just the ability to hit the right note.

Pastor Dallas Wilson is a long-time friend of mine. He shared a story with me one morning concerning his two youngest children. He said that they were in the back seat of the car arguing with one another on the way to school like most kids do. That wasn't very unusual but what was unusual is what they were arguing about. They were fighting about who would win a fight between a crocodile and a panther. Dallas complained to me about how ridiculous the argument was and then paused to ask me who would win. The answer is what blessed us both. It all depends on whose atmosphere that they are in. If they are fighting on the land, then the panther would win but if they are fighting in the water then the crocodile would win. The moral of the story is that we must make sure that our worship is led by the power of God's Spirit because it produces a Kingdom atmosphere where the devil cannot survive. Use the Spirit of God to give you the power to worship.

CHAPTER 7
HOLY SPIRIT MY STANDBY

"I, John, your brother and companion in the suffering and Kingdom and patient endurance that are ours in Jesus, was on the island of Patmos because of the Word of God and the testimony of Jesus. On the Lord's Day, I was in the Spirit, and I heard behind me a loud voice like a trumpet, which said: 'Write on a scroll what you see and send it to the seven churches: to Ephesus, Smyrna, Pergamum, Thyatira, Sardis, Philadelphia, and Laodicea'" (Revelation 1:9-11 NIV).

You will never really appreciate the content of John's letters until you first understand the context in which he was writing. First of all, John is an apostle who walked with Jesus from the very beginning of His ministry. He has forsaken everything that he had, including concern for his own physical life to follow Christ and His mission. He is now one of the last living Apostles and is about to face his own death. Biblical historians have suggested that John has escaped death at least three times at this point in his life.

The first time he escaped the sword of Herod. According to historians he then was placed in a boiling pot of olive oil but every time he would go down supernaturally, he would float back up. History says that no matter how much they heated up the oil he refused to die. He would miraculously rise back up to the surface. I don't know how accurate the story is, but it makes sense to me. Anytime the enemy throws the

Believer in the anointing we will always rise to the top. The last time that they decided to kill John they exiled him to an island called Patmos, chained him to a rock so he would die of a lack of food and loneliness. But what they did not know is sometimes it takes being pulled away to a place of solitude to get God to endow you with divine revelation. After all of the enemy's attacks, abandonment and mistreatment John yet had peace. How did he do it? It's right there in verse 10, "On the Lord's day, I was in the Spirit." He found his peace in the Spirit. He knew that although God would not deliver him from this season of pain, he could yet have peace because he knew that God was standing beside Him. He found peace in the presence of God's Spirit. I'm about to say something to you that you probably don't want to hear. God does not always deliver you from your storms immediately. Sometimes He just gives you the grace and peace to sustain you while you're in it. As a matter of fact, sometimes God gets more glory out of your life while you praise Him in it than He gets when you praise Him after it. But He has promised each one of us that He will never leave us alone.

Genesis 1:1-2 says, "In the beginning, God created the heavens and the Earth. Now the Earth was formless and empty, darkness was over the surface of the deep, and the Spirit of God was hovering over the waters."

This passage gives us a fairly vivid description of the creation story. It talks about how empty, dark, and chaotic the world was before God transformed it. It is also a shadow of the depravity of man and God's process of transforming us. Before we met Jesus, our lives were empty, dark, and chaotic but the Father spoke light into our lives and totally transformed us. Look closely at verse 2. "Now the Earth was formless and empty, darkness was over the surface of the deep, and the Spirit of God was hovering over the waters." Notice that the Spirit of God hovered over all of this chaos. The Word hovered there literally translates BROOD. Like a mother hen broods over her eggs. The mother does this process of brooding for two reasons. One to incubate the eggs so that they will hatch and reach their full potential and the other reason is to protect the eggs from predators. That's what the Spirit of God does for us. He nurtured and incubates us so we can reach our full potential in Christ and He covers and protects us from the devil's devices so that we can live life more abundantly. He is our great "Stand-Byer." His very presence brings us unimaginable peace.

There's a famous story that preachers use all over the country about the undying love of a grandfather. I can appreciate it even more now because I have now become one. The story is told of a first-time mother that had a six-month-old baby. The baby was the cutest thing that you had ever seen but she had one major problem. She was spoiled rotten and refused to let you put her down without screaming at the top of her lungs. The mother knew that she had to break her from being held, so no matter how loud the child cried she refused to take her out of her small playpen. The baby cried and cried but the mother refused to pick her up. After about 15 minutes granddaddy came in and immediately picked the baby up and of course, the baby stopped crying.

The daughter walked out of the kitchen and told granddaddy to put the child back in the playpen because she was trying to train the baby. The mother made granddaddy promise her that he would not take the baby out of the playpen no matter how much she cried. Reluctantly granddaddy agreed. Mom goes back in the kitchen and now both the baby and granddaddy are crying. After about 20 minutes mom realizes that she doesn't hear her baby crying anymore. She had a pretty good feeling what had happened, Granddad had taken the baby out of the playpen and broken his promise. But to her surprise, he hadn't. He didn't have the baby out of the playpen he had literally climbed inside the playpen with the baby. You see God doesn't always get us out of the things that we want him to get us out of, but He always sends His Spirit into the difficult places with us. He is always close enough to us to hold us in His arms and wipes the tears from our eyes. His Spirit will always be with us even in the scariest times of life. "For the Spirit God gave us does not make us timid, but gives us power, love, and self-discipline" (2 Timothy 1:7 NIV).

CHAPTER 8
HOLY SPIRIT MY TEACHER

Just this morning I was talking with one of my spiritual daughters who has just finished her doctorate degree in Anthropology. She said that after graduation the Lord blessed her to be a professor at a college in Dallas. She was so excited to share with me about her students and their growth in the classroom. She said that the lowest grade that she gave this semester was 100. I told her how proud of her that I was and how blessed I was to have her as a daughter. She said Dad, I didn't say that I earned the 100's but that the students did. I shared with her that the quality of the student is always predicated upon the investment of the teacher. You can never make withdrawals where someone has not made a deposit. Did you know that it is also true about your spiritual life? If you have achieved any sort of spiritual success in any area of your life it is because some faithful teacher has made investments into you. Maybe it was a Pastor, Sunday school teacher, Christian mentor, or prayer partner but someone needs to be honored for the part that they played in your spiritual growth.

However, the greatest teacher that you have had according to the scriptures is the Holy Spirit. He is the one that deserves to be honored the most for all of His revelation, divine wisdom, and spiritual insight. I know you usually don't see the Holy Spirit as a teacher, but He definitely is. He is not just working on your heart to love like Jesus or working your hands to heal like Jesus, but He is working on your mind to think like Jesus. Let's look at how the Holy Spirit is described in the scriptures and it will bring clarity to my point. Matthew 3:16 NIV says, "As soon as Jesus was baptized, he went up out of the water. At that moment heaven was opened, and he saw the Spirit of God descending like a dove and alighting on him."

Here the Spirit comes in the form of a dove but look where it lands, on Jesus' head.

Psalm 23:5 NIV says, "You prepare a table before me in the presence of my enemies. You anoint my head with oil; my cup overflows."

Here, the Spirit comes in the form of oil but look at where it lands, on David's Head.

Acts 2:1-4 NIV, "When the day of Pentecost came, they were all together in one place.

Suddenly a sound like the blowing of a violent wind came from heaven and filled the whole house where they were sitting. They saw what seemed to be tongues of fire that separated and came to rest on each of them. All of them were filled with the Holy Spirit and began to speak in other tongues as the Spirit enabled them."

Here the Spirit comes in the form of tongues of fire and once again, look where it lands, on their heads. I think that what the Holy Spirit is trying to teach us through the placement of His presence is that He desires to make an impact on our minds. He knows that whoever has your mind holds your destiny. Therefore, the dove, the oil, and the fire of the Holy Spirit have been intentional about engaging our minds, thoughts, and wills so that He can teach us the things of God. Everything you need to know about your God, yourself and your assignment can be found in the Holy Spirit, but you have to see Him as more than one who excites you but also as one who instructs you.

If anybody knows me, they know that my iPad is my life source. You rarely will catch me without it. It is the tool that I use to navigate through all of the important things that I need to get done. Hundreds of written sermons are on it. All of my important contact information and emails are on it. All of my business contracts and documents are on it. Most of my pictures and video from foreign mission trips that I took throughout the world are on it. All of the books and curriculums that I have written in the past are housed there. I'm even typing the words of this chapter on it. It is simply a very significant tool that I have gotten accustomed to using that makes me much more competent in life. When I lose it, which seems to be fairly frequent here lately, I become overly frantic and anxious until I eventually find it. Sad to say but it has literally become my mind in an electronic box.

My 8- and 10-year-old sons have also become somewhat attached and dependent upon it. However, not for email access or sermon preparation. They don't use it for the exegesis of a Greek word or the reminder of a doctor's appointment, but they are addicted to the iPad for a completely different reason, the games! You see we both use the same piece of property but for two different purposes. I use it as a TOOL, and they use it as a TOY. The thing that determines how we both use it is the level of our maturity.

There are so many people that only see the Holy Spirit as a toy. Something to make you feel good temporarily or something that can be played with in a way that makes a person look powerful and important. This is a sign of spiritual immaturity.

God wants us to use the Holy Spirit as a tool to teach us all things and to give us wisdom into His will for our lives. So many people have used the Holy Spirit as a toy so often that many people don't even believe that He is still relevant to the Christian's life. But listen to me my friend, He is still as relevant to our lives today as He was in the days of Jesus and the apostles. If you will open yourself up to the leading and learning of the Holy Spirit you will gain knowledge and insight that you could only imagine. "But you have an anointing from the Holy One [you have been set apart, specially gifted and prepared by the Holy Spirit], and all of you know [the truth because He teaches us, illuminates our minds, and guards us from error]" (1 John 2:20 AMP).

Did you hear what John said in the (c) clause of verse 20, "and all of you know [the truth because He teaches us, illuminates our minds, and guards us from error]?" All that simply means is that if you allow the Spirit of Truth to teach you, He'll give you the discernment to know when you're being lied to so that you won't find yourself in error. Wow! I'm getting excited about that truth even while I'm writing it. The Holy Spirit has an uncanny way of giving you a clue to when you are being manipulated into error. Have you ever been about to make a decision that was either business, relational or even something pretty insignificant where everything looked right on the surface but something in your gut wouldn't let you rest or move forward? Never ignore that gut feeling, it's generally the Holy Spirit throwing red flags at you because He sees something in your future that you can't see while you're still in your present.

Trust Him, He's always right. Even if you get the "unction" at the altar in your wedding dress listen to Him and run the other way. Even if you get that "unction" while signing the contract on that new home, walk away. Even if the U-Haul is already loaded and you're in route to another city. If you get that kick in your gut, unload the truck, say you're sorry and continue to follow the voice of God. Trust me it would be better for you to tell those that will be disappointed with you sorry today than to ignore the unction of the Spirit and be disappointed for the rest of your life. Although you don't understand it now, God does and if you will keep seeking after Him, He will eventually reveal His will for you in His timing.

"However, as it is written: 'What no eye has seen, what no ear has heard, and what no human mind has conceived' — the things God has prepared for those who love him— these are the things God has revealed to us by his Spirit. The Spirit searches all things, even the deep things of God. For who knows a person's thoughts except for their own spirit within them? In the same way, no one knows the thoughts of God except the Spirit of God. What we have received is not the spirit of the world, but the Spirit who is from God, so that we may understand what God has freely given us. This is what we speak, not in words taught us by human wisdom but in words taught by the Spirit, explaining spiritual realities with Spirit-taught words. The person without the Spirit does not accept the things that come from the Spirit of God but considers them foolishness and cannot understand them because they are discerned only through the Spirit" (1 Corinthians 2:9-14 NIV).

About 33 years ago one of the most powerful fights of all time took place between a man by the name of Iron Mike Tyson and Trevor Berbick. It was deemed as one of the most viewed sports events in history. Celebrities and stars from all over the world had gathered in Las Vegas to see if the 22-year-old Mike Tyson would be victorious over Trevor Berbick and become the youngest heavyweight fighter of all times. I was told that

Mike looked as though he was at the top of his game in both his skill and health as he entered the ring with just a towel around his neck, black boots, and no socks. I heard that he had rage in his eyes as he stared Trevor down during the referee's preliminary rules. Notice that I keep using phrases like I heard, and I was told. It's because I didn't get to see the fight. It's not that I did not plan to see the fight, or I was not prepared to see the fight but in the process of watching, something major went wrong.

A close friend of mine decided that we would both watch the fight, but we would watch it from our own homes. He would just call me when the fight came on and we would commentate back-and-forth with one another. Well just as the clock struck 8:00 p.m. the bell rang, and the fight had begun. My friend said, "Man did you see that right hook? Did you see that jab to the face? Did you see that uppercut to the ribs? I don't think

Trevor is going to make it through this next round." After he paused for a second, I was finally able to let him know that I didn't see any of the fight. I could only see snow on my television and could only hear the sound of static in the background. Evidently, I had put my TV on the wrong channel. I asked him, what channel are you watching? He said channel 102. That was the exact channel that I was watching. I then asked what time did it come on? He said, 8:00 p.m. That's exactly what time I cut my television on. How can we be watching the same station at the same time but yet he is able to see that which I could not? He then asked me this question, man do you have cable? In embarrassment, I said to him no, I don't have cable. He said how do you think you're going to see what I'm seeing when you are not hooked up to the same power source that I'm hooked up to? Even if we're on the same channel you'll never be able to see what I'm seeing if you don't have cable.

Guess what family, when you received the Lord as your Savior it didn't just come with Christ, but it also came with Cable. You received the Power of the Holy Spirit that allows you to have insight and vision that other people can't see. Therefore, it is foolish for you to continue to try and explain to those that are in their flesh what God is showing you in the Spirit. "For the message of the cross is foolishness to those who are perishing, but to us who are being saved it is the power of God" (1 Corinthians 1:18 NIV).

Continue to learn from the Holy Spirit. Allow Him to be your teacher in all things and you will graduate Summa Cum Laude from the University of Adversity. God has promised that "The Spirit of the Lord will rest on him— the Spirit of wisdom and of understanding, the Spirit of counsel and of might, the Spirit of the knowledge and fear of the Lord — and he will delight in the fear of the Lord. He will not judge by what he sees with his eyes, or decide by what he hears with his ears" (Isaiah 11:2-3 NIV).

CHAPTER 9
THE HOLY SPIRIT MY REMINDER

We have learned that the Holy Spirit has been ordained in our lives to be our teacher. However, no good teacher sits down to train a student in a particular area or educate them with a particular skill without also preparing a test to see what they have learned.

Jesus spent countless hours with His disciples as He walked with them for 3 1/2 years, teaching them everything that He knew. He taught them how to handle people who were caught in the traps of sin. He taught them how to heal people who were hurting both physically and spiritually. He taught them how to continue to love and care for people who would never love them back. He taught them how to maintain peace in the middle of storms and He even taught them how to die for the Kingdom and yet maintain their integrity. Everything that Jesus taught His disciples as they were walking with Him in these 3 1/2 years, He was doing it realizing that one day they would be tested on the lessons that He taught. He needed to see if they would, in fact, remember what He had taught them. Because again, what's the use of spending precious time in a classroom, teaching students if there's not a test to validate the process. I can hear the voice of my 6th-grade teacher now saying, students, you better pay attention to my instruction because if it comes out of my mouth then it's going to be a part of your test.

I often tell our congregation, whenever you are in Church don't allow anything to distract you because everything that is being said from that Word you are responsible for, whether you are paying attention or not. If it comes out of God's mouth, it's probably going to show up in a test that is coming your way.

"All this I have spoken while still with you. But the Advocate, the Holy Spirit, whom the Father will send in my name, will teach you all things and will remind you of everything I have said to you" (John 14:25-26 NIV).

If you will just ask the Holy Spirit, He will remind you of everything that the Master has taught you when you face those tests. He's your cheat sheet. Nobody should continue to flunk a test if they have a cheat sheet in front of them. But you have to depend upon the Holy Spirit to remind you.

On the other hand, I will never remember something that I have never heard. That is why it's so important to get into the Word of God and make it a daily discipline in your life so that even if I do forget what God told me, the Holy Spirit will bring it back to my remembrance at the very time that I need it.

Remember the Covenant

One of the things that the Holy Spirit reminds us of is our covenant with God. The word covenant refers to a binding agreement between two or more parties. God has established many covenants with His people throughout the Bible but the greatest one is the covenant of salvation. It's a covenant that comes with unbreakable and irreversible promises. Let's look at Ephesians 1:13-14 for a moment so that we can appreciate the magnitude of the covenant promise that the Father has made with us. "In Him, you also, when you heard the Word of Truth, the good news of your salvation, and [as a result] believed in Him, were stamped with the seal of the promised Holy Spirit [the One promised by Christ] as owned and protected [by God]."

First of all, our covenant promise was based solely on His love for us and our acceptance of that love. The moment we believed, He immediately cuts covenant with us and seals us with His Spirit. The words stamped and sealed were carefully chosen by the writer to make sure that we understand the terms of the covenant. It's a homily or image of a person who has an important document that is only validated through an official seal, stamp, or signature. Much like the seal or stamp that is on a marriage license. Regardless of whether a couple has exchanged rings, had a wedding ceremony or even sexual intercourse that couple is still not legally married until the marriage certificate has been officially stamped by the State government, placed into an envelope, and sealed by the proper authorities.

When God saved you, He signed Your name in the Lambs Book of Life, He sealed you with the power of the Holy Ghost and delivered you out of darkness into His marvelous light. Now that's something to sing about. We are signed, sealed, and delivered! Verse 14 says, "The Spirit is the guarantee [the first installment, the pledge, a foretaste] of our inheritance until the redemption of God's own [purchased] possession [His believers], to the praise of His glory."

This verse uses a parabolic analogy of a person who is in the process of purchasing something of great value such as a business, a building, or some sort of real estate. He says that the Holy Spirit was the pledge or first installment of our purchasing cost. I remember when my wife and I were in the process of purchasing our first home. We had finally built our credit up to the point where we had gotten pre-approved. We had identified the particular neighborhood that we wanted to raise our family in and then we finally found the perfect house. It was a 3-bedroom wood home trimmed in mountain stone. We were so excited yet so full of anticipation that we didn't know what to do. We decided to move forward so we made an offer. The only problem was that two other families were also making offers. The stress of the process began to really take a toll on us both emotionally.

Our realtor noticed our anxiety and asked us what our fear was. We told her that we didn't want to lose the house to another family because we believed that's where God wanted us to live. She then stated, well if that's the case then put your earnest money down on it and take it off the market. I didn't realize that we could put a portion of the purchasing price down as a down payment and it would take the property off the market so no one else could get their hands on it. When Jesus died for us on Calvary's cross, He made this statement, "Into your hand, I give my Spirit", then He gave up the Ghost. What He was doing is putting a down payment on our salvation even before He paid our sin debt in full. He wanted to make sure that He took us off the market so the devil couldn't get his hands on us.

The Holy Spirit was then and still is now, our earnest money and guarantee of all that comes with our covenant. Your covenant promise comes with more than just eternal life when you die. It comes with some great perks even while you're still living. It comes with joy, peace, hope, forgiveness, prosperity, health, wholeness, freedom, community and so much more. But not only that, when we leave this Earth the Lord promises us that we will be completely free from the power, the presence and all of the penalties of sin. The Word promises that in the twinkling of an eye we shall be changed into the very likeness of Jesus. Hallelujah! I can't wait until that promise is fulfilled in our lives.

Remember the Cost

Sometimes we don't appreciate our salvation because we forget about the cost that came with it. I mean let's just think about it. How many times have you heard a preacher or even yourself say that salvation is the free gift of God? That is actually only partially true. Salvation may be a free gift from God, but it definitely was not a free gift for God. It cost Him His most valuable asset, His only Son. Let's just be honest. How many of you would allow your child to die for someone that might or might not even love you for it? No really, let's put this to the test. Pull out your cell phone right now, go to your pictures and find that loved one that has stolen your heart. Is it your son, your daughter, your husband, or your wife? Is it that grandbaby or lifelong friend? Whoever it is, can you imagine giving them up to die a brutal death for the person that hates you the most? Of course, you wouldn't do it, and neither would I. But God did!

"As for you, you were dead in your transgressions and sins, in which you used to live when you followed the ways of this world and of the ruler of the Kingdom of the air, the spirit who is now at work in those who are disobedient. All of us also lived among them at one time, gratifying the cravings of our flesh and following its desires and thoughts. Like the rest, we were by nature deserving of wrath. But because of his great love for us, God, who is rich in mercy, made us alive with Christ even when we were dead in transgressions—it is by grace you have been saved. And God raised us up with Christ and seated us with him in the heavenly realms in Christ Jesus" (Ephesians 2:1-6 NIV).

Because God knows that we can get so caught up in our own personal affairs and the cares of this world He sends the Holy Spirit into our hearts to remind us the extent of His love towards us. Whether you agree or not we need the Holy Spirit to constantly remind us of the price tag that was hanging from the cross. Our souls did not come from the local Goodwill Store down the street or off some clearance rack in a closing mall. Our souls were hanging from the most expensive rack in hell and Satan refused to sell us cheap. So, when we are complaining about how long the Church service is and how it's making us miss the first quarter of the football game, we need to be reminded. When we are tempted to hold a grudge against someone who owes us a few dollars, we need to be reminded. When we are mad at God because He doesn't give us everything that we put on our spiritual Christmas list, we need to be reminded. When we complain because the sacrifice of the call that is upon our lives and we threaten to quit, we need to be reminded. Remind us of the 3-inch thorns that were pushed into His brow. Remind us of the railroad spikes that were driven through His hands. Remind us of the chunks of human flesh that were stripped from His back from the brutal beating. Remind us of the blood and water that gushed from His side and remind us of the heat in hell that His soul endured while being mocked by the devil himself. We need to be reminded. Holy Spirit never let us forget the cost of our freedom in Christ Jesus.

Remember the Consequences

I've learned that Satan does not just desire to create so much confusion in my life that I lose my mind, but He also wants me to lose my memory. The times that I have been tormented the worst by the devil is when I had lost my memory. Give me a moment to explain and I think this will bless you. One of the characteristics of the devil that most theologians agree on is that he is a master of manipulation. He's an expert at playing mind games on his victims. That's what he did with Eve in the garden, David in his bedchamber with Bathsheba, Judas in the upper room at the last supper and with you every day. He plays with our minds to try to convince us to do what is wrong and make us think that it's alright. That's why Romans 12 cautions us not to be conformed to the world but to be transformed by the renewing of our minds because that's how satan gets his advantage by and through manipulation. John 10:10 says that the enemy comes to kill, steal, and destroy and the thing that he wants to steal the most are your memories. But not all of them, some things he never wants you to forget.

Satan's plan is to get you to remember all of the fun that you had when you were serving him. But he wants you to forget the consequences that came after all the fun was over. Proverbs 26:11 NIV says, "As a dog returns to its vomit, so fools repeat their folly." When dogs eat their vomit, they are re-eating that which made them sick in the first place and then become even sicker when they eat it again. Why would they do that, because they remember how good it tasted but they forgot how sick it made them. Hasn't the enemy done that to you before? Hasn't he ever reminded you of how good it was when you were in your mess, but he intentionally forgot to remind you how much it cost you? He'll remind you of the great times that you had in that relationship, but he won't remind you of how you almost lost your life trying to get out of it. He'll remind you of the wild parties and late nights of the past, but he won't remind you of DUI charges and the time that you spent in jail. He'll remind you of the great sexual experience and fantasies that you fulfilled but he won't remind you of the fear that you had of being pregnant. The devil has a great mind, we have a terrible memory and that combination often times leads us to a world of trouble.

I believe that there is something embedded in the hearts of all of us that periodically desires to go back to the bondage that God has brought us from. It's something that is connected to our old nature that we have to fight every day. It's usually triggered by a major let down in life. It may happen after the death of a loved one. It may be after the loss of a job. Sometimes after a conflict with a Church member. It may even happen because of an unanswered prayer or after the disappointment of self but all of us deal with it from time to time. Lot's wife wanted to go back into Sodom after the Lord destroyed the city. The children of Israel wanted to go back to Egypt after crossing the Red Sea. The Galatians wanted to go back to the law after they had experienced God's grace. Peter went back to fishing after the death of Jesus and even I as a Pastor of a thriving Church have been tempted to go back to the world in times of discouragement.

All of us are tempted to go back to something but here's the good news you don't have to go. 1 Corinthians 10:13 NIV says, "No temptation has overtaken you except what is common to mankind. And God is faithful; he will not let you be tempted beyond what you can bear. But when you are tempted, he will also provide a way out so that you can endure it." I personally believe that one of the ways of escape He gives us is that internal voice of God warning you not to make the same mistake that you did the last time. Don't listen to the enemy reminding you of all the fun that you had when you were in your sin. Listen to the Holy Spirit remind you of all the hell that you went through while you were in it. Listen to that voice that sometimes is not a scream but more often a whisper reminding you of how God loves you and how He desires for you to live a life that pleases Him.

People praise God for all sorts of things these days. They praise Him for houses and land. They praise Him for prosperity and promotion. They praise Him for family and favor and none of them are bad reasons. However, lately, I've been praising Him for the still small voice of the Holy Spirit reminding me of how good it is to live in the perfect will of God.

Remember the Call

Every person that is reading this book is reading it for a divine reason. You didn't pick this up by accident or coincidence but by God's divine providence. He has purposefully led me to write about the Holy Spirit and He has also purposefully led you to read it. God has a purpose that He has entrusted you with and He has given you everything that you need to fulfill it. It may not be a call to preach, or Pastor or anything that is connected to Church ministry, but you yet have a calling that He needs you to accomplish. If you were not necessary to the ultimate plan of God, He would have never allowed you to be born and definitely not born again. If you still have a pulse, then you still have a purpose. The Holy Spirit will not just reveal your calling to you, but He will empower you to walk in it.

"His divine power has given us everything we need for a godly life through our knowledge of him who called us by his own glory and goodness. Through these he has given us his very great and precious promises, so that through them you may participate in the divine nature, having escaped the corruption in the world caused by evil desires" (2 Peter 1:3-4 NIV).

All these verses are saying that we have no more excuses of why we can't be used by God, for His divine power has endowed us with everything we need for success.

I remember being called to plant our ministry over 16 years ago. Every time that God tried to tell me what He wanted me to do I rebutted with an excuse, and they were pretty good excuses if I may add. Lord, I would but I don't have the money. I would but I don't have a building. I would but I don't have the people. I would but I am not smart enough. Lord, I would but I don't have the resources down here to do what you want me to do with success. Lord, I feel powerless. I was too spiritually immature to know that that was exactly where God wanted me, empty, inadequate, and weak. I guess I had forgotten all of those sermons about faith and trusting God. I had just preached to a small crowd the week before from the subject of THE WEAKER THE SERVANT THE STRONGER THE SAVIOR. But let me be honest it's always a lot easier to preach it to others than live it yourself. God quickly taught me that His strength is made perfect in my weakness. I was looking for my strength in people, places, and things when I should have been looking to the hills from where all of my help comes from.

I told this story in another one of my books, but I think that it is worth retelling. In late October of 2012, a major hurricane hit the northern portion of the United States. It really did a job on New York and New Jersey. I was actually on a cruise in Jamaica when it happened. However, because I had both family and friends in the line of the storm, I watched every moment of it on television from the ship. It had consumed every news station. I don't think there was a great loss of life, but multiple millions were lost in property damage. Some were left without lights or power for almost two weeks. At the climax of the storm, both New York and New Jersey had lost all power and were left in complete darkness. It was eerie to watch. New York City with all of its high towers, skyscrapers, and electronic build boards with no power. The cities were pitch black.

As I continued to look, I noticed something strange. There was a small light flickering in all of that darkness. It was extremely tiny but extremely bright especially sitting on the canvas of the blackout. As one of the CBS cameras zoomed in, I figured out what it was. It was the Statue of Liberty. In all of that wind, lightning, and rain that girl still had her hand up and was still letting her light shine. There are two things that I learned that night. No matter how bad your storm gets, keep your hands up in praise and let your light shine before people no matter how dark it gets. Never allow your storm to get the best of you. In all things give thanks for this is the will of God concerning you. Never ever let the devil put your light out.

But how was she still shining in the middle of a storm that had knocked out all of the power? How could she remain as bright in the storm as she was before the storm hit? I found out later when I got home. I asked a friend of mine that is a nerd at heart. I said how could the statue of liberty in New York still have light when all of the power was out in the entire city. He said it's because that Statue of Liberty doesn't get her power from New York she gets it from Philadelphia. The point that I'm trying to make is this. Often times we don't walk in our callings because we know that it's going to take power to make it come to pass but we can't see where it's coming from. What God wants us to do is stop looking for the power from down here on Earth and know that our power comes from somewhere else. It comes from Him in Heaven. The one who spoke into darkness and called out the light. The one who spoke those things that were not, and they became. The one who formed the worlds with His Word and they never have stopped existing. The one who formed man from the dust of the Earth and breathed the Spirit into His nostrils and man became a living soul. Stop thinking about your weakness, your lack, and your deficits. The power of the Holy Ghost will anoint your mission and see you through.

CONCLUSION

As I bring this book to a climax, my prayer is that you have become more acquainted with the Holy Ghost who is the God in you. My prayer is that you will embrace Him fully in all His Glory just as you have received God the Father and God the Son. He has been waiting on you to fan His flames in your life and take a deeper dive into His power. Know that He will be your comforter when you have lost all hope. He will be your advocate when the odds are stacked against you. He will be your intercessor when you're standing in the need of prayer. He will be your counselor when you need guidance for the journey. He will be your strengthener when you feel like you're at your weakest point. He will stand beside you when everyone else has walked away. He will be your teacher when you feel like you're flunking the test and He will remind you of everything that the enemy wanted you to forget. May God's Spirit find you, fill you and forever set you on fire from this day forward.

Challenge to the Church

I was taught very early by my Pastor, the Late Reverend H. H. Wright, that a preacher should never give divine revelation without challenging the listener to the application. What he meant by that statement was that if the Word of God does not move us to transformation then it ultimately will become no more than an exercise of futility. The challenge that I have for the Body of Christ is to use the revelation that is found in this book to release the Holy Spirit to improve and empower your life. Jesus tells the story of a woman who entered into a house that He was having dinner. He reclined at the table; the woman approached Him with an alabaster box full of precious expensive oil. She took the box, broke it, and poured every ounce of the valuable oil upon the Master. She refused to keep even one drop for herself. Not only could you smell the fragrance of the oil on Jesus, but the fragrance literally consumed the entire house.

I believe that Jesus shares this story so that we will know what He expects from us as it pertains to our stewardship of the Holy Spirit. We must first realize that the oil of the Holy Spirit was never given for our own selfish ambitions but was given for the mission of Christ. Secondly, the Holy Spirit was never designed to be used one drop at a time and then saved for special occasions. He is to be poured out completely and liberally every day of our lives. Thirdly, the Holy Spirit will never fully be appreciated or activated in the Kingdom until we allow the Father to break us and get Him out of the box.

And lastly, we will know that the Holy Spirit has truly been poured out in the Earth when the fragrance of the anointing begins to change the environment in which we live in. It must bring tangible impact to the rearing of our children, the pursuit that we have towards justice, the generosity that we show in our giving, the decisions made in our government, the compassion that we display to the weak and the light that we shine into the darkness. "And afterward, I will pour out my Spirit on all people. Your sons and daughters will prophesy, your old men will dream dreams, your young men will see visions. Even on my servants, both men and women, I will pour out my Spirit in those days" (Joel 2:28-29 NIV).

HOLY SPIRIT IGNORED NO MORE

A FORMAL INTRODUCTION TO THE GOD IN YOU

DEVOTIONAL

CHAPTER 1
THE PERSON OF THE HOLY SPIRIT

Do you generally think of the Holy Spirit having a personality when you think about Him? What do you think has shaped and developed your definition of the Holy Spirit?

What are some of the personality traits of the Holy Spirit that were mentioned in this chapter?

Which one of them means the most to you?

How can you begin to react to the Holy Spirit in a more relational way?

Why do you think that many people ignore the person of the Holy Spirit?

How can you begin to address the Holy Spirit differently in your prayer life?

How have you seen the Holy Spirit benefit your life lately?

What do you think that the consequences would be if the Church became more intimate with the Holy Spirit?

How will you take what you have learned in this chapter and apply it to your life?

Who do you know that needs this revelation concerning the Spirit and when you will you share it with them?

CHAPTER 2
HOLY SPIRIT MY COMFORTER

Name a few words that come to mind when you hear the term comforter.

Describe a time in your life that was so difficult that you couldn't be comforted by people?

What are some things that people run to when they are struggling with discomfort?

The Holy Spirit promises to be our comforter. How has He brought comfort to you in the past?

What did you learn in this particular chapter that perhaps was a little surprising?

Why do you feel that sometimes we refuse to allow the Holy Spirit to comfort us?

What will you do as a result of reading this chapter to benefit from the comfort of the Holy Spirit?

Who do you know that needs the Holy Spirit to bring comfort to their lives and how will you share this revelation with them?

CHAPTER 3
HOLY SPIRIT MY ADVOCATE

What are some words that you would consider synonyms with the word advocate?

Have you ever considered the Holy Spirit to be your advocate?

Have you ever felt like your sin destroyed your relationship with God? Explain that feeling?

Why do you think that we so often believe that God does not love us?

How does it make you feel to know that the Holy Spirit is advocating for you to God?

Describe a time when your guilt was so overwhelming that you almost gave up on yourself?

How did you recover from your guilt?

Now that you know that the Holy Spirit is speaking on your behalf to the Father, how will you respond to Satan's words of condemnation?

What was the most important lesson that you learned through this chapter?

How will you live your life differently after reading this chapter?

Who do you know that is dealing with guilt or shame? How will you share this knowledge with them?

CHAPTER 4
HOLY SPIRIT MY INTERCESSOR

What are some of the hindrances to your prayer life?

Why do you think that God makes prayer such a priority in our faith?

Have you ever felt like you just didn't know how to pray or what to pray about?

How will you approach God now when you feel empty in prayer?

Have you ever witnessed blessings show up in your life beyond what you had prayed for? Explain.

What are the most important lessons that you have learned through reading this chapter?

How will you apply the principles of this chapter to make you a better Christian?

How will you begin to partner with the Holy Spirit in your prayer time?

CHAPTER 5
HOLY SPIRIT MY COUNSELOR

When you hear the word counselor what other words come to mind?

Share a time when you felt like you were completely lost and without direction.

How did you eventually recover from it?

This chapter teachers us that the Holy Spirit is a counselor. How have you seen the Holy Spirit bring direction and guidance to your life?

A counselor cannot be effective until the client is willing to submit to his direction. Why is it so difficult for us sometimes be submitted to the leading of the Holy Spirit?

Describe a time when the Holy Spirit told you to do one thing, but you did something else? How did it impact you?

Ephesians 5 challenges us to be filled with the Holy Spirit. Have you ever felt like you had been depleted of His presence? Explain how?

The Holy Spirit wants to completely control us and influence every decision that we make. What area in your life do you have the greatest problem giving up control and why?

Explain a time when you submitted your life to the leading Holy Spirit. What were the results?

What was the most important thing that you've learned from the chapter?

How will you apply these truths to your life from this day forward?

CHAPTER 6 HOLY SPIRIT MY STRENGTHENER

What are some areas in your life that you feel weak in?

After reading this chapter how will you rely on the Holy Spirit to strengthen you?

Do you struggle with sharing the gospel with others?

What is your reservation when sharing the gospel with others?

How do you feel when you read that the Holy Spirit will give you power to witness?

What are some temptations and weaknesses that you have that you need the Holy Spirit to give you victory over?

Describe a time when the Holy Spirit gave you power over your weakness and how did it make you feel?

According to this chapter, how does the Holy Spirit impact our worship?

What were the most significant points that came from this chapter?

How will you embrace the Holy Spirit in order to receive more power?

CHAPTER 7
HOLY SPIRIT MY STANDBY

What was the most interesting point to you in this chapter?

Describe a time where you really needed to know that God was present in your situation?

Try to explain how the Holy Spirit expresses His presence in your life.

Peace generally accompanies the presence of God. Explain a time when you were in the middle of a storm, yet the Holy Spirit kept you in peace.

How will you cultivate your relationship with the Holy Spirit as a result of this chapter?

Why do you think that we seek the help and presence of people before seeking the presence and assistance of the Holy Spirit? How will you resist the temptation of running to people instead of depending on the Holy Spirit?

How will you share this truth with others so that they can rest in the presence of the Holy Spirit?

CHAPTER 8
HOLY SPIRIT MY TEACHER

How has the Holy Spirit been active in your life?

What part of this chapter spoke to you the strongest?

What has the Holy Spirit taught you about yourself?

What has the Holy Spirit taught you about Himself?

In what areas do you need the Holy Spirit to mature you in right now?

Describe a time when you heard a Word from the Lord and then shortly after you were tested on it?

How did you respond to the test?

How will you apply what you have learned from this chapter?

CHAPTER 9
HOLY SPIRIT MY REMINDER

What are the major points that came from this chapter?

What did you learn about God's covenant with us?

What does it mean that we have been sealed with the Holy Spirit?

What does it mean that the Holy Spirit is our down payment and how does that impact you personally?

What was the cost of your salvation?

How does that impact the way that you serve God?

Describe a time when you returned to a sin that you were delivered from?

How did it impact your life?

Share a time when the Holy Spirit reminded you of the consequences of sin and kept you from yielding to temptation.

What area of ministry is the Holy Spirit pushing you into?

When will you start walking in your calling?

What was the most significant point in this chapter and how will you apply it to your life?

ABOUT THE AUTHOR

Pastor Daryl W. Arnold is the Founder and Senior Pastor of Overcoming Believers Church in Knoxville, TN. He and wife, Lady Carmeisha Arnold, are divinely called to inspire believers to live abundantly, and to empower them to walk in the fullness of their kingdom authority.

While known nationally for his revelatory preaching and his passion for the Word of God, setting atmospheres of worship, and winning souls, Pastor Arnold is also passionate about serving the Knoxville community, committed to "Reaching Out Around the Rest" with outreach ministries, services, events that have impacted thousands of lives.

Pastor Arnold is a member of Kappa Alpha Psi Fraternity. He serves as the first Board Chair for Girl Talk Incorporated and currently serves as Co-Chair for The Change Center Board of Directors. He serves on the Knoxville City Mayor's Save Our Sons (S.O.S) Task Force under the umbrella of My Brother's Keeper initiated by President Barak Obama. He's a Task Force Member for the Knox County School Superintendent for Disparities in Educational Outcomes. He's on the Steering Committee for Community Connectors Knoxville under the umbrella of CEO's for Cities Nationally. He is a graduate of Leadership Knoxville Foundation where he currently serves on the Board.

Additionally, Pastor Arnold serves on the Johnson University Advisory Board as well as a board member of the Trinity Health Foundation. Pastor Arnold is a graduate of Leadership Knoxville Foundation and has recently taken on the role as a member of the Leadership Tennessee Foundation. Pastor Arnold is the author of *There's No Place Like Home.*

A native of Chattanooga, Tennessee, Daryl's greatest joy is his beautiful wife of 24 years, Carmeisha Arnold, and his four children and granddaughter. His hands are on his ministry, but his heart is on his family.

OTHER REV/12 PUBLICATIONS

In *There's No Place Like Home: Discovering the Destiny Within*, pastor and teacher Daryl W. Arnold unpacks biblical truths that will encourage and empower you to pursue your God-given destiny. Using the classic story, *The Wizard of Oz* and its unique characters, Pastor Arnold paints a picture of the journey we all take as we discover God's purpose for our lives, the challenges we experience on the way and just how deeply this journey changes us. This combination book and study guide, designed for individual or group reflection, will not only encourage and entertain you, it will provide practical steps toward pursuing the abundant life God has for you, a life that far exceeds anything you could ask for or imagine.

In Ephesians 6, Paul is writing a letter to the Church of Ephesus encouraging them to stand firm as they go through some of the toughest times in their Christian journey. He is first acknowledging that God has confirmed their salvation, empowered them to be victorious, and called them to greatness yet they will still have to overcome the schemes of the devil in the process. The Apostle Paul uses the image of a Roman soldier's armor as a tangible example of how we can arm ourselves against the evil one. Through this Inductive Teaching Series study guide, pastor and teacher Daryl W. Arnold's prayer is that the study of these scriptures will prepare you for spiritual warfare, propel you into your God given purpose and prevent you from giving up during the process.

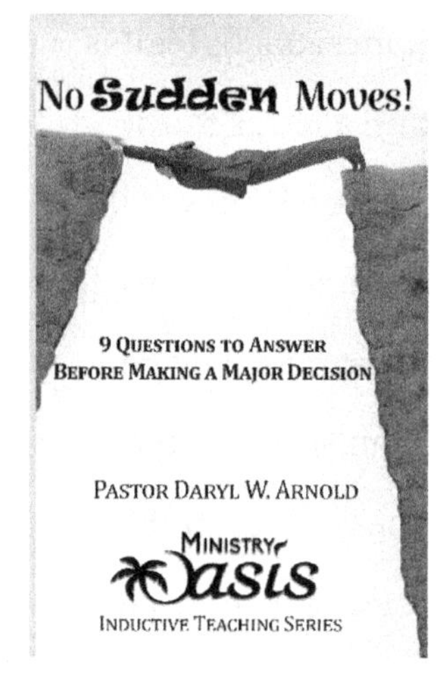

Life is a series of decisions that need to be made in order to fulfill the purpose God has prepared for us. The problem is that sometimes knowing what decision to make can be hard to discern and sometimes even harder to do. Prayerfully, this Inductive Teaching Series will equip you to lean on these 9 steps of wisdom to assist you in moving in the right direction. No matter how anxious you may be to make that decision, resist the temptation to move forward until you have answered all 9 of these critical questions.

Christians throughout the world often use the blood of Jesus to overcome their adversity but neglect to use their testimony as a bridge to their breakthrough. *The Word of Our Testimony - Treasures from Broken Vessels*, is a series of short topical devotions that are written with the purpose of bringing encouragement to the discouraged, hope to the hopeless, help to the helpless and to once again set the fire of faith to those who feel spiritually burned out. Allow these candid testimonies from broken men, women, and children of diverse backgrounds to stir up the gifts of God that have been lying dormant within.